A CATALOG OF FUTURE MERCIES

Also by Serena Chopra

Ic

This Human

A CATALOG OF FUTURE MERCIES

Poems

Serena Chopra

Graywolf Press

Published by Graywolf Press
212 Third Avenue North, Suite 485
Minneapolis, Minnesota 55401

www.graywolfpress.org

Published in the United States of America

ISBN 978-1-64445-396-4 (paperback)
ISBN 978-1-64445-397-1 (ebook)

2 4 6 8 9 7 5 3 1
First Graywolf Printing, 2026

Library of Congress Cataloging-in-Publication Data

Names: Chopra, Serena author
Title: A catalog of future mercies : poems / Serena Chopra.
Description: Minneapolis, Minnesota : Graywolf Press, 2026.
Identifiers: LCCN 2025049996 (print) | LCCN 2025049997 (ebook) | ISBN 9781644453964 trade paperback | ISBN 9781644453971 epub
Subjects: LCGFT: Poetry
Classification: LCC PS3603.H673 C38 2026 (print) | LCC PS3603.H673 (ebook)
LC record available at https://lccn.loc.gov/2025049996
LC ebook record available at https://lccn.loc.gov/2025049997

Cover design: Luis Vázquez O'Neill

Cover art: Courtesy of the author

I weave these strands into a breathing basket. I imagine I am reweaving the passageway for neurotransmission. I massage each strand with rose oil, whispering to future light impulses: *don't drop the signal.*

—SELAH SATERSTROM, *RANCHER*

Contents

PART III

PART IV

A CATALOG OF FUTURE MERCIES

PRELUDE

In the nervous wheat, the wind

Are there sounds of pain in the night

from a distant corner of your home?

the psychic asks.

Yes.

Durations of absence of sound   tense we, like tensions lay

tethered to our beds, nerves
tethered to the darkness tethered
to the looming notes, chilling
like a limber prairie wind sucked
into the panes of our shelter.

It is, the psychic sees,

Dayawati—
come to offer mercy.

I

Seduction, after the Great Plains

Across the stage, a birth chart of weightless deviations, each body

filling itself on a canon of lusting—constellate me, untense me, give

me into the last-resort sinew, bone at the cool glory

of my sexy clarity, stop-motion as a strobe-lit prairie.

Watch me watch me in the mirror—lag lines of an evaporated spill.

O lightning, water is furious conjunction: I arch sternum and spread leg, know better

than to keep dearly in the empty pockets of pussy commodity.

I take copper under my tongue, wade the pool,

channel the nightshift through an electric plain of roving mothers—

meaning, under the stench of men and cigarettes, I am foul-mouth blood, a whole world

laid wet with pearl, so

when I dance you read what you can see, my eyes

turned beneath heaving light-caught rhinestone on lashes

is a spin   a swerve   a veil.

I'm not here with you or for me; I cut this circulation of barter and tend.

I bring tender, I do better, I lick the wound and enter—

letting the tongue split and wander there.

The Signal

One may never know
how fully proximal
they are to pain—

began the story of many lives, our own.

I shelter what survives survival, I collect you
in the thick nerves of ghost town—listen, that haggling
between weather-sore structure
and collapse.

The world falls away from us
like meat from the bone
as they say of good meat on blackened bone
as they say of widows on the pyre—

your mother
on the father
in the fire
that made you

mercy, Daya

do not be afraid of our wounds, it is forgiveness
that cannot hold a truth stable.

Lick the wound and enter

But which of us wants to remember

the emaciated nerves

of an unwell future

fraying like rope

around its fits of knot,

its rhizome of wild grass

roped in the lawn.

Leather Shoe

: You said there was a story, Dad?

: Yeah, there's a—a—before I was born.

Amber flinch of wild grass in your evening eye.

Steady claws of a trembling machine: memory
digs, heaves rhizome, knotted in clots of clay.

Excavation's imprint, afterimage
of the machine that, breaking you, heaps.

It's a saying. It's just a saying. When people get mad, they say it—
they'll say, "I'll make shoes with your leather!"

It's a threat that means to kill someone and make leather shoes with the skin.

So, like, if they decide to kill you and make leather shoes out of it—um
It's just an analogy, a saying—just that kind of thing.

Dadi | Grandmother

Birth: Early February 1920, Patiala, Punjab.

Name / नाम	Daya / दया Dayawati / दयावती
Meaning / अथ	Mercy Full of mercy

In principle: *Daya*
does not forget the tragedies of the world.

Daya confronts tragedy, uses one's means to drown
suffering. Offers breath

compassion sympathy kindness *mercy—*

Daya suffers in sympathy with, having pity on
breathlessness, becomes herself
breathless

suffers suffering
in the suffering of all others.

Daya observes alien pain [ropes, fire, addiction, madness—
Daya moves [with caution, asthmatic
with affection [lactating, shoeless, breathless
toward the sufferer [begging *daya, daya, daya*
to the river

to act mercifully [to drown this suffering
with kindness and forgiveness— [forging breath for giving,
forgiving
breath
breathlessly.

Rather than tolerate others' death, one imbued with दया
Daya
chooses herself to die.

That I am anger Are you hunger That broken flower pot
still begging for **water** A season in smoke in ice in the sunlight
Suffering **comfort** The medicine that clearing **me** That beast
of great sequins Where I call myself out to the night And
morning already pruning herself **into waking** Escapist nature
Suffering ordinary **constellations** Originate shapes Fingers
kneeling against teeth Flora heaving strange inspiration In a vase
Possesses humans **All** which flaws Folding hands, lips
Suffering teeth I **may** be the golden **decay in you**, the water
In which leans rootless, our favorite bouquet

Water, comfort me
into waking constellations—
all suffering may decay in you.

Marriage: 1934; bride given to Anand Sagar Chopra, son of Mrs. Malavi Devi Chopra; cash & jewelry dowry [1 wedding sari & set of 8 gold bangles to be kept by bride as insurance]; bride, 14 years old, illiterate.

Name / नाम	
Meaning / अथ	Mercy

to have to one's name, to have it taken—

Dictation:

saas	सास	mother-in-law
dahej	दहेज	dowry
rassi	रस्सी	rope

For example:
Dahej rassi kee tarah baandhta hai | दहेज रस्सी की तरह बांधता है।
Dowry binds like rope.

Saas ne rassi se Dayawati ko mara | सास ने रस्सी से दयावती को मारा।
Mother-in-law hits Dayawati with rope.

Rassi ke lie Dayawati | रस्सी के लिए दयावती। Mercy for the rope.

Home Practice:
Malavi Devi ties the knot, strikes Dayawati—ruptures ((knots of sound)) *mercy* the eardrum ((deaf ness *Daya* full of— sound
drowned sound
ringing stolen ((sound)) of one's name drown—

Now, sound it out.

Strike from one, their name—
in the name of the laws
of the mothers of sons
procuring daughters.

(sound out)

It is also practiced:
Who ties the knot
takes the firstborn son.

I open you **in my hand** on the ground and am counting with you, the retreating steps.   The sweetness of burnt onion, garlic on fingertips to remind you **your agility** with a blade, with slick skin. The knotted rope against your ears, your deafness the inexplicable diagnosis of mine. **Our** legs **braided** with muscle bend like baskets conveying—   the **intimacy** of resting in your own strength, the love you wheeze between your breasts, I imagine these were your **rituals** too.   I imagine the silence left you **no forgiveness** and the tinnitus in my ears is the strain of your crisis, swallowed and packed neatly in your jaws

In my hand, your agility—
our braided intimacy
rituals no forgiveness.

Breath: By 1944, Dayawati lost three children.

In the first, a daughter.
Four years old, reason unknown (unremembered).

take copper under the tongue, channel night
through an electric plain of roving mothers

In the second pregnancy, Malavi Devi persuaded Anand
a woman must be disciplined to be depleted
of her sorrows.

know better than to keep dearly
in the empty pockets of commodity

In the second, Daya spilled milk she pulled from the cow
and was lashed. Took slim rest and was lashed. Made bitter tea
and was lashed—

arch sternum and spread leg
a blade, your slick skin

In the second, she fled to the Tapti river.
She took two wrong trains and was lost for days.

the world falls away like meat from the bone

Witnesses reported her tattered, lactating, haunting the stations,
shoeless as a beggar.

give into the last-resort sinew

She took by foot and train to the river. In the second, who pulled
her from the river—

jaw clenched, knotted throat,
a stolen state of calm

In the second, Daya's breasts, flooded with river, fed the child
desperate water.

what survives survival—

In the second, it was anyway only another daughter, emaciated leather.

watch me watch me in the mirror

In the third, it was relayed to Daya that if she bore a son,
Malavi Devi would take him as her own.

O lightning, water is furious conjunction

It was confirmed the infant would be taken directly after depletion
of breast milk.

stop-motion, strobe-lit prairie

It was said there could be visits when the child grew older.

lick the wound and enter—

In the third, Daya dreamed of a bridge, impossibly rivered.

a whole world laid wet with pearl

In the third, a great pain of water broke, bearing
a pearled son.

tongue split and wandering

And waking in laudanum delirium, her son already stolen
from her still-wet breast—

the wound entering and entering

In the third, she refused to empty herself of the pain—her breasts
full of hardening pearl. But this, her only wager, did not match
the certain threat of rope—

ritual of no forgiveness

She pulled from herself as she pulled from the cow, pouring ghost.

lag lines of an evaporated spill

In Afterimage

Dowry death is often the murder of a wife by suicide—

hanging, drowned, self-poisoned and sleeping
in railroad tracks, her eyes slice

blade of night train blaring
moon glazing everything

suddenly delayed.

: Dad, you said there was a story.
How to weigh a hand for its mercy—

Of what we remember to tell, what is left to show—time developing
unforgiving questions in the afterimage.

Our eyes watch between us, as if a mirror eclipsed
by the red drought of wound.

I collect things collapsed: eardrum, artery, airway, mind—our
nuanced anatomy of suffocation.

In utero, we become according to what we cannot contain.
Cutaneous from the beginning, and aglow.

: Yeah—before I was born—one night, she got—my mom wanted to, uh—left.

You cough, extracting an artifact of breathlessness.
Your hands rest on the table, knuckles lace a single tension of fist.

She went to the Tapti River—and then somehow she—something happened.

We grieve the prairie hard-pressed into its fractures. Our thirsting
nerves like roots reeling split land. We toe the line of fault.

She was pregnant with—and she decided—with me, I think—yeah, so she got
onto this—um, she was somehow—she had no other place to go.

In *pregnant*, a root to *praise, celebrate, sing*; and another to *heaviness—the weight of grief.*

We stumble to unearth her suffering, tremble any resemblance—
her nerves pregnant in the grieving heat between our hands.

But we can only imagine Dayawati whipped in the mud, fissure
of eardrum, a flight of thin red ribbon, damp sound inhumed.

She was beaten—with knotted ropes—

Deafness pregnant with tinnitus, aching chorus
of granddaughters wheezing.

: A saying. It's just a saying.
A saying. It's just a saying.

: She fled to her father's house. He said, "Go back! You're their property.
It's up to them if they decide to make their shoes out of your leather."

: A saying. It's just a saying.
Just a saying.

Rope braided from darbha grass; rope twisted from the anjan tree.
Used for balancing buckets or heaving feed or tying cattle or—

: When she got fed up, she wanted to jump from—from the bridge, in—into the river.

Bride of drunken manias and catatonic spells, a child.[1]

As a young ecosystem, prairies appeared out of climatic duress
forming unprecedented preservation technologies. *No, no—*

She didn't want to go back into that hell again. She went straight to the train station and decided to go to Nagpur where my dad's older sister lived.

But she couldn't read and—
Dayawati full of lost children.

she took the wrong train and instead of going south, she went north.
Her arms arched over empty, over ghosts—

1. To be a child bride before the Dowry Prohibition Act (1961, India).

In her arms, ghosts—to chase to where to flee—

She had no money on her she had nothing. She didn't get any food, nothing—
by herself, devastated—Without shoes!—that's what, uh, people said that—

The dust of a step
stained with blood.

The journey was three days to Nagpur, but she was lost for weeks,
pregnant with—and running

along the riverbed, you gaze the emptiness out our window,
land split-pregnant with the phantom of future homes.

But—this, uh, was actually—it was not me. This was her fourth pregnancy.

You recall the muskmelon farmers in April, resurrecting
their plots from the receding river. The bank, a cross-section

of drowning. It's true, some might compare a fetus to fruit,
but in actual imaging, it's like an ear turning into a lung.

Ready to hang heavy
on its own breath.

Lungs like ears filling with heartbeat, the heart heavy with—

: A saying. It's just a saying.

: But this was not me. I forgot—the, a, him—

In utero, in the final weeks—lungs and fat—respiration becomes
a boundary, one's light transparency turns opaque—

lungs fill with rhythms used later for speech.

My aunt refused to return my mother. She wrote to my dad—
that he needs to get his act together and move to Nagpur. So, my dad went

but he came unwell—your hands speak, pucker and point, *Sores*—
flowering around his mouth—

Who held her breath
when he entered

Mercy, lungs spreading like grieving light on water.

Symptoms include: enlarged, rashed, swollen, collapsed.

In utero, in the final weeks, syphilis spread to the fetus.

And he was in so much pain before he died. He was like three, four years old.
I was only two and even I remember him suffering.

Mere Dada Ji | मेरे दादा जी | My Grandfather

A fault is a lineage of catastrophe—

Tectonic rage, erosive surrender.
Rain shadows depriving land of water.
Fractured jaw of knuckled quartz.
Magma's insidious brain. Stone
exhausted soft.

On the vulnerable plain, lightning
enrages drought. But we
can only imagine
a healthy need
for fire.

Of what we remember to tell, what remains to show—slouched
defense of bone. Leather resurrected in cobbled knots.

My grandfather constructed roads and bridges, hired hands, hundreds
to build concrete roads to the Ajanta Caves and two bridges in Bhusawal

for crossing the Tapti River during monsoons.

Named for the goddess—*hot one*, *burning one*—Tapti wheezes
with droughts fierce as her floods.

Daughter of sun and shadow: No one in three worlds, they say,
could match Tapti's devotion.

Sun heats her dark deception; watery shadows break light,
incoherent spitfire of glittering embers.

No one
so whole.

But any story of bridges descends from chasms.

And any story of prairie portends unforgiving seasons. The rattle
of drought (death) and katydid (mating) camouflages snakes (preying).

I was afraid of seeing him. He used to chase me down . . . [coughs] . . . uh—but we had everything—servants, a big house—a famous house—The Chopra House.

My father bought his first camera when he was seventeen.

Only one photo remains of The Chopra House, haunted
with the afterimage of a developing accident. *He set fire to—tossed gasoline*

and set fire . . . [inaudible] . . . but nobody realized it—that he had a problem.
He was not diagnosed. It was not his fault.[2]

My ears fill like the lungs of a hyperventilating brain.
I decipher Daya wheezing in the tinnitus of my lost hearing.

He showed his affection in a different way. Like, he'd take me to the toy store and say, Buy whatever you want!—so, so—

But he didn't treat my mom very well.
She suffered a lot.[3]

Even in deafness, the rumbling blur of anger

the rhythmic plunge
of attack.

---

2. To suffer disorder before existing diagnostics (Manic-Depressive Illness, *DSM-II*, 1968).

3. To be a woman before the Protection of Women from Domestic Violence Act (2005, India).

The Chopra House | Bhusawal, Maharashtra, 1965

Twenty-two capricious rooms.
    The mood swing of intricate tiling.
        Delusions winking from gold-leaf ornamentations.
            Corridor echolalia of slamming brass locks.
        Insomnia of skeleton keys.
    Gregarious banisters swooning manic fits of stairs.
Breathtaking atrium, passing out the long gaze of unglazed windows.
        Curtains hiding children.
    Highs ceiling lows.
Cold, agile milk door—quick escape, a flight
    of roof-terrace stairs without rail.
        Great lungs of banana leaves rattling the wind.

I developed asthma. I was very bad. And she was very bad; my mom was very sick, too.

Both of us—we used to gasp for air.

Pain circles the concentric circles of pain. The debts of mercy
swell fetal in my lungs. I cannot breathe

these stories. I gasp at their air, excavate burials of lost breath.
I reach arms over head, spread my lungs like the jaws of a storm.

I wheeze and you pat your hip for an inhaler.
You stretch to retrieve it from your blue jeans' pocket

as when I was a child and, at the slightest predawn wheeze,
your sleep frayed, echolocation—your instinct still listening for

your mother. You'd rush to my bedside with the prototype inhaler
that immigrated with you from India.

Airway closure during an asthma attack is not, as it is in drowning,
closure as self-preservation. Rather, it is collapse caused by a trigger,

a body suffocating itself from the inside.

You'd unwrap the worn cylinder box from a cloth and pull from it a
glass tube extended like a crooked finger from a brown rubber bulb.

With one hand on my back, you held it to my lips and coordinated:
counting three, squeezing the bulb, *breathe*—counting three, squeeze,

breathe—rest—*breathe*—rest—

Then, noticing your own breathlessness, would hold the yellowed
glass to your lips, smiling to ease our mutual worry. *Breathe*, rest—

Sighing, we'd sit together confirming our breath, our debt
of breath—our subdued wheezing peeling us off the crickets' night.

Ears like lungs fill the brain. Sound hemorrhaging in the wounds
we've made between us. Our pain circles the circles of her pain.

I circle you, your eyes in the archive of afterimage. You search,
extract a small wheeze, trailing like a lost lyric, a chip of vocal rune.

I circle you, circling: long hallways, heavy doors, echo—echolalia
like apology. Lungs collapsed on the drums of manic laughter, home

suffocating itself
from the inside.

: It's just a saying, a saying—just

A house full
of breathless.

: I remember running after my mom because, you know, there was a fight
or whatever it was, and she just said, like, "I'm going to kill

myself." And she just runs out of the house, you know. And we were kids, you know,
were like really devastated with that—and so—so I ran after her.

I was young, not even in high school. I'm running after her and my little sisters were crying
and, you know—it was that kind of scenario.

And she, you know—I couldn't find her, it was night, uh, totally pitch dark.
And I was running, calling her name and finally caught up

with her. You know, then I brought her back. Uh, but—but it was like that
all the time.

: You'd find her at the edge?

: Yeah, near the river, yeah. She was threatening to kill herself. I mean,
not threatening—she wanted to. She wanted to kill herself. She was trying to jump

off the bridge—the bridge my dad built—off, in—
into the river, she—

She was just going—yeah—she was going—

Dayawati draws water from the bed of her suicides, slaps
clothes brittle against its hot rock banks,

sleeves flailing like drowning limbs
hung from the anjan trees.

Site at the blooming imprint, vanishing

In the ash shadow of wildfire: fireweed blooms—

flushed rhizome, feathered seeds of psyche

don her charged pyre.

My cells flare with apparition,

a low storm in every joint.

Site: Séance

A photograph—taken in 1984 in Aurora, Colorado—of Dayawati and me was unearthed in 2015, the same year that I started writing this book and that I also mysteriously developed tinnitus, mild deafness, and vitiligo (pigment depletion) in and around my right ear, directly where, in the photo, Dayawati stares. Suddenly there, I grew a shock of white hair. In 2018, in séance with the photograph, I heard her whisper between the ringing in my ears, guiding me to divine signals she imprinted in the photo, during my first summer and her last. The signals arrived subcutaneously, like vitiligo and like certain species of prairie flora emerging from thirty-year-old rhizomes or inhumed seeds, nursed by deep wells of ancient water.

The Prairie Hands Me a Love for Time-Under-Vacancy

i.

In our only photograph, we wear white.

Behind us, an empty riverbed runs into the road
breathless

between us

the riverbed traces a signal: What is depletion—
A prairie, a prayer, an edge spreading.

ii.

The riverbed is a rupture, a seam reaching—

Behind Dayawati, prairie. Behind me, a fenced-in lawn.

In our origin photo, the sidewalk ends behind our back one time runs out of another.

iii.

In our only photo, between her lips
is a word on the tip
of my tongue.

iv.

Prairie water is hard, signals séance.

Mercy holds her granddaughter electric to the current—
          Phantom flare of fireweed sears a seam between us: flares in my ear, a phantom scar.

                    The river haunts her prayer: durations of absence of sound
          notated by telephone lines
running into the future—
                    Look where Dayawati looks. Watch the sun there. Watch for it
                    in thirty years.

In my ear in thirty years, I grow a deafness,
I grow a ghost.

Vitiligo: of cutaneous trembling,
of an etymology tracing *blemish*,
tracing *vice*, *fault*, *guilt*.

v.

Guilt is a knot inside a knot—inside her fist, mine.

How to weigh a hand for its mercy.

Let them make shoes of your leather.

The rope used for balancing buckets or heaving feed or tying cattle or
of rupture ringing—

A saying, a saying.

One good ear kneading the other's silence.

Subcutaneous trembling—
In our origin photo, my blood at both ends of the rope.

vi.

In our only photo, everything is new except Dayawati the prairie the mountains running out of breath.

Vitiligo: of blemish, of vice, of fault.

Of fault: an extended break
in the body.

vii.

An extended breaking-in the body.

Our tongues tie trying
to articulate the knot.

A word, a knot of her leather.

In our photo, if we make mercy
of her leather—

viii.

As if to fault my hearing in her shadow and my pigment in her sight—
As if her gaze pours vision into my eyes—

A prairie spreads beneath the lawn, haunts the lawn a ghost.

ix.

I hold stone fruit, hardened fruit, the many-faced fruit imprinted in my palm: I hold the rudraksha around her neck.

In our origin photo, the prairie like a prayer running out
of breath.

x.

My arm across the tightness in her chest: a mother slamming
the brakes.

Vitiligo:
bruise of an extended ghost.

xi.

Dayawati whispers mercy
is a seeing, a sprawling sight.

A phantom flares between us.

Watch the sun there. Watch for it in thirty years:
of deafness, depletion blooms vitiligo
around my ear, white hair
like a thirty-year prayer
like the milk of a punctured weed
like a riverbed-dusted road
like rhizomic faults
in the lawn.

xii.

In thirty years, I misspell it "*vita*ligo" because I sense depletion is elsewhere life—

xiii.

In our origin photo she holds me where once her blood and once her water and once her leather held her breath. Where once she held children losing breath.

In our origin photo, holding our breath holding
in the sun between us, her mercy, her many-faced fruit.

xiv.

In drought, deep roots of prairie species seek ancient water sites.

There is a ghost muscle that is water, there is her rage there there is the fear of lifting her to our lips, of letting her act upon our cells—

Mercy: the wound resurrect listens, pulls her milk
weeds into the lawn.

Vitiligo:
of Dayawati, I am a fault.

xv.

Her eyes like no eyes like aspen eyes like knots
like branches full-bruised of dormant
buds like what grows over despite the dead
are ghosts unrelenting.

xvi.

In our origin photo: the prairie's edge—fenced-off penumbra of clay edging   rusting nails
edging thirsting edging   lawn edging   petrified and mica edging   sidewalk edging   dust
storms caught in gutters and neatly drained
of séance—

Of our origin
signal
blooming

Dayawati
full of—

hear hear
a ghost.

Myth of the River, Hungry as a Knife

A river came upon a mare in the shadow center of a woods. The mare was an illusion that the shadow coveted. The mare tasted her lost name in the river. And to the river the shadow whispered, *Daughter?*

Before the mare lost her name, she was woman: a mother, a wife married to the sun of a brutal world. Unlike the mare, the shadow carried with her her own name—Chhaya, "nimble shade."

Chhaya fell into the mare's eyes, turning their amber amnesia black. The well of their sight cradled Chhaya in infinite familiarity, as that between current and tide. The warm river came onto the mare's tongue filling her with *maa—*

Mausi, Maan

The mare tasted from the river a fiery monsoon and held it in her jaws. The mare tasted from the river and found her name, Sanjna—"quick and nimble"—like a wet relic on her tongue. Then, in her great mare lungs, the hum of *Chhaya* ached like velvet, a pain caught like lint in the fine-haired nerves of memory.

The mare remembered herself as Sanjna, remembered herself the wife of the sun god, Surya. Sanjna couldn't handle the heat of her master and his domain so she fashioned an illusion, a shadow twin, a sister cool enough to handle being handled, and named her Chhaya. Then, Sanjna slipped into the night, leaving her children in Chhaya's cold embrace.

•

Chhaya is the night walking through herself, nimbly, cooly into Surya's hot bed. By him, she begat a daughter, whom she loved more than Sanjna's abandoned children. For this unequal love, Yama—the lord of justice—daily abused Chhaya, unaware she was the shadow of a long gone wife. He kicked her, beat her with ropes, hid her daughter from her.

One day when Yama stood to kick her, Chhaya cursed his legs with flesh-eating worms. The curse revealed to Surya and Yama that this was not Sanjna but her shadow sister, a dark illusion—O, how shadows deceive and corrode justice! As Yama's legs began to fall away, Chhaya disappeared, a shade enshrined in shadow. Her beloved daughter turned into a river and followed her into the umbrage of a forest. Surya sent Loo, a hot demonic wind, to capture and return the daughter to him. Loo pursued the river, attempting to evaporate her momentum—but the river fled under an anjan grove, trees unbreakable even by fire.

Yet, in the heat of pursuit, the cooling river lost her mind, her name somewhere abandoned, sun bleached among the debris.

•

Lost, the river came upon a mare in the shadow-center of a woods. The mare was an illusion that the shadow coveted. The mare tasted her name in the river, to whom the shadow whispered, *Daughter.*

The shadow dipped herself into the river—*Daughter,* she pried again.

And unwinding from the umbrage, the shadow appeared to the river, her mother—*Chhaya Maan*, the river wept.

And remembering the mare into a woman, *Mausi*—mother's sister—*Sanjna Mausi*, the river yearned.

The mare watched the shadow sink into the river and wrap her daughter in a deep, warm shade. Chhaya fell into Sanjna's eyes, turning their amber amnesia black.

Daughter, Chhaya began, *You are Tapti—river ever returning to the home that burns her.*

O, hot one, burning one, Sanjna joined, *We are the mothers of your arrival: flight, illusion, and nimble shade. They will say no one in three worlds can match your devotion.*

But devotion to whom? Sanjna tasted from Tapti a fiery monsoon and held it in her jaws.
For they cannot hear the breath of granddaughters stirring the current
below your steadfast mirror gaze.

Tapti River | Bhusawal, Maharashtra, 1967

Tenants of an Untenable Mind

Bridge Construction over Tapti River (receded) | Bhusawal, Maharashtra, 1965

I. Flight, Illusion

"*Kharbuj* (muskmelon) is cultivated to a large extent on the sandy stretches in riverbeds. As soon as the river recedes and the sand banks are exposed, small plots are fenced off. . . . The melon beds commence fruiting in April and continue yielding, until they are covered by the swelling of riverbeds at the commencement of monsoon in June."

MAHARASHTRA STATE GAZETTEERS, GOVERNMENT OF MAHARASHTRA: JALGAON DISTRICT, 1962

Violence swells
dry seasons.

When the river leaves
her bed
bares itself like a vacant throat

In the dampness of absence,
a bridge ribbed empty of lung.

Memory strains to cut,   speaks scar   of the debris.

Fog signs the charge   of possessing
loss.

•

Excavation of a haunted bed—
Daya walks its sandy stretches, imagines the river in its long silk of sun—
imagines the river consuming her as it would the road: ferocious monsoon,
hysterical eviction, an unforgiving site.

She imagines the sluice
pouring her endlessly
of its un-anatomical self.

While her husband solves the river with a bridge,
Daya wanders relics of the river's flight—artifacts of failed attempt—

O how lucid, her brazen exoskeleton.

•

Or, a bridge impossibly rivered—

With monsoon at her throat, she leans
over the edge, a gold pendant
caught pendulous
by the sun.

Is insanity the bridge
or the monsoon bruising herself against it—

II. Flight and Nimble Shade

> *"Anjan—Hardwickia binata.*—This beautiful and graceful tree is found practically all over the district. The timber is excellent. . . . The bark yields a strong fibre which without any preparation can be twisted into rope."
>
> *MAHARASHTRA STATE GAZETTEERS*, GOVERNMENT OF MAHARASHTRA: JALGAON DISTRICT, 1962

What remains of memory in the weather of an untenable mind—

Of what I can assemble: My grandfather staring out our kitchen window, sunk steady as a wind-bent shed, displaced and drifting. Fingers resigned around the aura of a faded blue ॐ tattoo.

He stares the prairie—
Nervous wheat. Tension of few trees.

Memory like a sudden blade drawing-in the brown breath of rot.

Memory like hundreds of hands building a bridge toward his two hands
when once they drew sure a match and tossed it
like a contorted prayer into the gasoline they poured on the door
of a room with his son locked frightened inside—

O, mansion of a thousand failed homes.
The timber is excellent
and so easily twisted.

•

My father remembers his father covering, floor to ceiling, the corridors in mirrors. Wrapping everyone in his warping. Threatening to leap from windows.

His youngest daughter empties bottles replacing the liquor with water he cries angers breaks mirrors holds himself like a shard plucked in a knuckle gathering blood like the atrium of a blocked heart. He paints everything red, wears red kurta, *only.*

But soon, monsoon—
a damp mind presses from roots and drapes from the sky. The prairie sighs,
sheathes herself, refilling her depleted wells of drought-survival.

Tapti returns to her bed. The land swells, unearthing what of survival.

With one halving machete strike, the gardener kills a cobra.

A servant is sent to the bazaar for white kurta, *only*.

Dayawati drapes the mirrors in her saris and watches her husband for months,
between bed and sofa, sofa and bed—caught
in the veiled mirrors like a ghost.

•

Or, fleeing for safety, Dayawati with her daughters left
my young father for weeks to look after—
Laughter

means run.

Don't cross

hectic eyes.

Keep a key

on the inside

of every door.

Don't look

back—

II

Neeni haath, "sleeping hand," my young father nightly requested of his mother: to tuck his small hand in her sari, to rest his hand on her belly.

When he slept, she unraveled herself like a spool from the pallu,
leaving him, his hand cocooned.

Like flesh ripening in its rind along the bed of a fled river—

Muskmelon, dust fruit.
Cut open, slice-mouth
of ten-fingers' breath.

Bridge over Tapti Riverbed | Bhusawal, Maharashtra, 2017

Unearth What Survives Survival

On   the hottest   day   I traveled   to the dry   riverbed

I asthmatic   lay   in the dry   riverbed   pouring ghost

fragments   of   limbs of   plaster deities

crumbled   where once Daya   curled suicides   in the grassy banks

Could she pour   ghost   Could she   curl   like smoke, *Maan*

kya aap   theek ho?   is not   what my father said   breathless

my small father   breathless running   ran to pull   his mother out

away   from the river   away and   home

running out of   home   is where   we run

breath out running us   home

is where a breath

breathes less

Uncaged from night, a feral dawn

In a vacated correlative—absence to ghosts—we are chained

to the debts of mania

the way *devour* slips

toward *devotion*

like cats called-in from the coyotes

like a promise of geraniums

wilting in heat.

Mere Pita Ji | मेरे पता जी | My Father

My sister and I can laugh together for hours.

Our father disliked our laughter—*Enough!* he'd command, *Stop acting crazy—*

And quieter, we'd laugh harder between
us, at him, mimicking *crazy, crazy,*
crazy, rolling our eyes,
Stop being crazy—
Acting crazy, crazy, crazy—

Debt Occasions, a Prairie Lamentation

When he was nine, my father woke in a field to
the crack and holler of the other boys already
at their cricket.

Like other boys, my father loved cricket.

/

My father laughs to remember—

the smoke stutters/the roots stutter/the rain stutters
in the grass.

Like my father, I grew up listening to tallgrass.

We lived on American
Great Plains
in one of the first homes
of a suburban development
that, over thirty years, grew to consume
the surrounding prairie.

But in the '80s, from our back porch, my father relished lingering westward—
lightning, planets, golden land sighing mountains—a man arrested by the breadth of his escape.

Unlike my father, I had a father who never drank.

/

Divorce
spit home
in our hands,
rubbed them together.

I grew up a dark daughter of a dark father along a dry riverbed, on an ever-expanding construction site, playing house in unfinished homes, plucking milkweed from their plumbing, creeping through their skeletons, collecting rusty artifacts. I was determined to unearth an object of history, a fossil, an arrowhead, but all I found were bits of failed construction.

My father and I built a garden of prosperous mint and failed artichoke, and a lawn full of invasive species. From our kitchen window, I watched miles of prairie portioned into concrete foundations.

Like my father, I grew up listening
to tallgrass fading
into site—
run-on sentence: depletion by expansion—

In the heat of construction, I traced the uneasy poetry of building home.

I pay obedience

I place our ghost

I pray with my small my curled

heart full

of rope

Prairie waking
in concrete cracks.

Injured garden
where the failed heart

blooms soft
off the choke.

Home is where

/

O darkness, thin mania—remember
the anger jumping like laughter—

Don't abandon the afterimage
of tile-hived floor, ghost paisley
across your father's face—

O
if the poem is an occasion—is this
the occasion?

Once, I came upon a fawn curled in a crease of tallgrass, dark eyes bulged and buoyed like
the lump in my throat. When I cupped my hands over my mouth, his eyes lightened
and pressed at me like the caesura draining between my palms.

/

the smoke stutters/the roots stutter/the rain stutters
in the grass.

For weeks, the cobra tracking patiently its prey   can see   nothing   else

I fall easily into the poetry of brown eyes—that amber ache I call *long-looking suffered heat*

—named after the flight my father made into that foggy Maharashtra night
—named after the flames dimming in his irises as he hid, peering back

in the grass

Peering back—where home was   on fire   where   was home   is where the fire—

Peering back, the darkness suddenly swelled with the smoke of the fire quelled
by the servants hurling buckets of water—could he hear them still?
Or was it really so great a distance
at which he found himself, settling like an ember
into the grass

/

Never peer back
   at the violence quelled,
   at the emptiness stiffening,
   at the trace of event
abandoning you—

My father laughs through remembering, telling us the times his father—

And I feel guilty for ever remembering, for even thinking of the times my father—

All kinds of crazy times possess us, I guess. I rattle with alarm. I chew memory, spit—

Later in the car, my wife, devastated in the afterimage of his memories, mourns, celebrates—

How incredible it is you came to be—

Meaning, how many times before my conception, my father nearly—

And how, even before his conception, his mother nearly—

always was

How close to violence we master our love.

Once, my father lingered at the window, scanning the dusk spreading its shadow
over the prairie—

When behind him, his father locked in laughter, laughing,
laughter licking the edges of the locked door, drooling smoke, spitting fire.

When below, the gardener, with machete sheathed, lifted his arms to catch—

Once my father jumped he ran and
Once woke up in a field of grass

holler holler crack—

Mind-locked, broke key: my grandfather hunting
my father.

These lunatic sentences.
These knots in my throat.

/

I watched the fawn
in his little patch of long grass
curled close to the hectic road—

his dark eyes pressing me—

When—where was his mother?
When for safety, his mother—
her eyes tracking my scent falling
all around her fawn.

stutters
in the grass

Crack◂◂Before awakened in a field◂◂Before abandoned with looking back◂◂Before awakened in a field when ball cracked at the bat◂◂Before dreams knot between your ears◂◂Before what kind of abandon nears◂◂Before a father heavy in mind and fist◂◂Before what kind of narcotic night will let this child slip◂◂Before into sleep◂◂Before the darkness thinning thinned◂◂ Before your pupils punctuate black◂◂When peering back◂◂Before the quiet quells the smoke ◂◂Before is it o

Before it is over◂◂Before the smoke ghosted◂◂Before looking back, abandoned◂◂Before in the tall grass scanning—stars, snakes◂◂Before where◂◂Before when was the burning◂◂Before in the distance◂◂Before the buckets of water◂◂Before the servants yelling for water◂◂Before you like an ember settled◂◂Before you like an ember settling◂◂Before in the tallgrass smelling like smoke◂◂Before asthmatic and shaking and smelling like burning◂◂When settling low, lay lower◂◂Before expanding your lungs◂◂Before raising your hands to expand◂◂When pleading with breath◂◂When out of breath◂◂When running out of breath◂◂When running you are running and◂◂When is it

When is it real◂◂When the house is burning◂◂When it is really real◂◂When is the ground and the land landing◂◂When anywhere but near where◂◂When a father laughing and running because◂◂When from the garden wall should you jump◂◂When watching the fire prey on and on◂◂When servants scatter for water◂◂When where is your father◂◂When the second story is on fire◂◂When the servants are yelling for you for water◂◂When you mount the wall◂◂When the gardener lifts you◂◂When you are small◂◂When you need to mount the wall◂◂When you hear your father laughing◂◂When which way out of the garden◂◂When where◂◂When there is your father, run!◂◂Look—

When looking up◂◂When the light could be dusk or flame◂◂When there must have been pain ◂◂Before landing in the garden◂◂Before caught hot in the grass◂◂When ejected like an ember, you are falling◂◂When falling wake up you are falling◂◂When like fire spitting, you jump◂◂ When calling to you to jump◂◂When with sheathed machete the gardener lifts his arms ◂◂When should you follow smoke out the window◂◂When from the second story should you jump◂◂When and shhh

When and should you jump◂◂When two stories up◂◂When locked in a room filling with smoke◂◂When the servants start yelling◂◂When flames are spitting◂◂When you've locked yourself in◂◂When from under the door, fire preys◂◂When preying on and on you◂◂When you've locked yourself behind a roaring door◂◂When twisting the hot key◂◂Before the door roars◂◂Before your father laughs◂◂Before he tosses the ma

Before he tosses the match◀◀Before he laughs◀◀Before he spits fire◀◀Before he douses the door ◀◀Before the servant is hit because◀◀When the servant objects◀◀When your father commands him douse the door with gasoline◀◀Before he calls for the servant and gasoline◀◀Before his anger is jumping like laughter like fire◀◀Before the door

Before the door shakes◀◀Before he pounds the door◀◀When he spits fire◀◀When you can't understand his anger◀◀When you back away from the door◀◀When you listen for◀◀When you shake the key the lock into place◀◀Before the lock punctuates its place◀◀When you shake the lock into place◀◀When you slam the door and shake◀◀When you can't understand his anger◀◀When the shards scatter◀◀When he is chasing you with laughter, puncturing the mirrors◀◀When you run◀◀When he punctures you with anger◀◀When spitting fire◀◀When he preys with fire◀◀When across his face the afterimage malaise◀◀When preying on and on you ◀◀When look quick from the floor◀◀When you count the tile floor in patterns of four◀◀When he sees you◀◀When he's drinking◀◀When he is and you are◀◀When for safety, your mother—

When where was your mother, Father—

(Heat in the leather   bends its broken—

Shoe stutter, creasing—

/

[deer]

O   doe

I rest my ghost.

/

And I feel guilty for ever remembering, for even thinking of the times my father—

Wakened in a field of depleted body

Deer,

I called animal services.
I reported your fawn

in his little patch of prairie curled close to the hectic road

eyes tracking me, my scent
falling all around
your fawn.

Step away they told me, *Step away.* Don't
trigger abandon.

My father came to visit me when I was on the edge, literally leaning on the edge of a blade when he knocked, slicing through the thick draped dramatics of my desperation, severing completely its integrity. He had never before *stopped by*, never *checked in*—these were the duties of daughters at which I was failing. His visit implied as much. He had never been to my apartment, and I am not sure where he got the address. Did I imagine letting him in? I remember his eyes skittish with embarrassment at my decor which is best described as *sapphic*. He sat uncomfortably at the table avoiding the breasts and yonic paintings avoiding the shame of my red and famished eyes. He could see I couldn't hide I had not really tried to move the sapphic out of me. The apartment frayed about us like a caged animal. I steadied the knife I sedated the air I soothed the minutes ticking on and suddenly I was offering my father tea trembling with the sudden confused reality filling suddenly the kettle. I excused myself to the bathroom to hide the knife patient in my pocket and knocked over a ceramic vase my late aunt had made—it broke, I broke and screamed I didn't want to die but I didn't think I could harbor myself any longer. From the table, my father calmly inquired after what was happening. I couldn't explain speech broke my veins were buzzing with a fever unequal to the day full of sun and easy traffic. I couldn't locate reality I grabbed at it breathless and crazed I found glue and arranged the broken I held determined to make them stick I can't remember if he watched but as I steadied the pieces together I gathered my father was in my home for the first time and what a maniac I had been. Why had he come. I had forgotten to turn on the flame, the gas clicking, clicking. He said he didn't want tea, he had to go, don't light the kitchen on fire and that I shouldn't get so worked up, it wasn't healthy. *Are you alright* is not what he said. He left a bag of food and advised an onion—*The servants would cut one in half and place it under her nose when my mother would get like this*, he gestured around the apartment, wrinkling his nose as if between the architecture, the familiar scent of a woman harboring her mercy in decay.

And I feel guilty for ever remembering—

What got child services involved was a curb check.

My high school English teacher called in the bruise.

Still, she likes to recount the story at parties, whenever we get together:

> *Serena comes to school—and this is twenty years ago—with a black eye—not funny, but this next part is—so I call my sister for advice. I say,* A student came to school with a black eye. Do you think I should say something? *and my sister says,* Why would you say something? I don't think it's any of your business. *Taken aback, I ask her,* Don't you think I should report it? *My sister replies,* I didn't know you were like that. Why would you report it? *Offended by her judgment, I snap back,* I didn't know you were like that! Why are you so against reporting it? I'm worried about her. It's a black eye! *And there is a pause and my sister laughs,* Oh! My god! A black eye! I thought you said a black guy!

Everyone laughs, drinks   my face still   hot where   the fracture kept me

from laughing   for months.

And it may be funny but I'm not joking when I say he threw fruit at me.
I'm not being funny when I stress throwing food is a sign of grave disrespect.
I have laughed before when recounting
          my father throwing fruit at me, calling me *slut*,   *you slutty—*

In denim and Britney Spears summers, Father, how else to be American?

Paying and paying
obedience—

To be American is an occasion! And in our great plain suburbs I had only to wear what every girl wore. But my breasts, a centuries-long cliché—

domes of the Taj Mahal   marble geometric mother
proud breasts of Mumtaz   the emperor's favorite wife

For twenty years he built for her, cutting off the hands of his artisans so they could not reproduce her marble tomb.

He built for her, in her breast, her tomb.

Centuries later, a man folds a dollar on my stage, says *Indian women have the best breasts.*

That they say a woman's breasts
are genetic inheritance from her father's mother.

That my father's mother was milking the cow when   struck with knotted rope.

Sacred cow, holy milk.
Clean the marble with mud.

A mind is a tantrum of light turned opaque.
Between us, a grief of subcutaneous knots.

We tug each our own end of rope.

/

Home is where

I flinch

but the bruise refuses
the bruising, tired
of rising to each, to every
occasion.

stutters
in the grass

Father, you called but I did not return home.

In the heat of violence, uneasy obedience.

The key is hot
afterimage cut
into our palms

Home is where
to lock

/

once when i could not see enough of the bruising   my eye blurring
i watched for hours in the mirror nearing time to wake for school
my face numb-hollow empty as waning crescent moon hollow
as foundation-cut prairie waiting for a home   a place to put
raging   with lagging eye i caught only the speckles of bruise only the dew
of the violence flooding me

when i needed urgently a blooming bruise to speak to me our grief i
locked mind tenderly lifted my knuckles to my swelling i
marked the spot   where the speckles might fill their constellation
inflorescent consolation   in the mirror i measured eye under my fist i
have never been so obediently numb as when

i unloaded my fist on my swelling   twelve sixteen twenty blows
my proliferating fist calling in the bruise eye watching me watch
me myself raise fist against face the occasion   run-on into our sentence the
bruising full breathing into what had been done
beneath my father's beneath my father's father's beneath whose eye my cheek
whose fist my eye whose cheek my fist until pins-and-needles full of sleep
waking late to a numb alarm it hurt to reach i went to class in the quiet halls i
was only my face only what we had done   to call the bruise home

Enough of home.

We compress, come lethargic
into the morning-sigh scatter
of sweeping glass

. . . heat in leather heat in leather heat . . .

the period is on fire and preying
the page into a mouth.

And who will order the next sentence.
And who will put it out.

/

Clay grips roots like who's got time for tenderness
when swelling with thirst, drying to dust
in yet another angry season.

But broken earth is full of eyes and nerve.

stutters
in the grass

Mercy, a length of prairie cracks the concrete,
haunts the sprawling rhizome of our great, plain healing.

Dear,
Can we bring tender—
Can we do better—

Our bruise blooms
long-looking suffered heat
watching me watch me
in the mirror.

III

Seduction, after Nocturnal Prey

Flat flat land, dust in our eyes, staring at the lust of the mountains, western
interrogation of our flatness staring at the sun, staring at the black leaning at our windows.

To make inside that blackness a million dollars, a woman of cosmopolitan seduction
to whom I give my girlhood nickname and leave red kiss on the threat of night.

And to myself, a stolen state of calm: the icy purple lips of too-early crocus.
I always begin with the moon in each spiral.

I know that, leaning here as I am, in the lap of a lap dance,
I withstand a lineage, suffer some sort of guilty comfort.

Is it labor turns girl into woman? Is it
the thought of distant seasons?

I first knew of broke American women with yet another dead engine
before I knew what it meant for her kept in perpetual dowry.

Does this violence embarrass you? My body is a home woven
of a thousand razor-thin faults where the debts of forgiveness

are shadows suffered. The cool night tripping over crickets.
But we are still the immigrants who made it—quiet home, fences.

When coming home at 4 a.m. to a dead bird in the kitchen, blood
like a snapped seam of sequins, feathers and the cat already sleeping.

Guilt, what nest have you made in my throat, feeding
from the winter keep of my heart?

Deepest discipline

Distance surrenders antelope

in an electric fog of hooves.

O rhizome, laboring creature,

listen the signal: life

grazing the nerves

of the earth; roots roused

from the farthest recess

of my deepest discipline.

Invasive Species

Father pulls at the prairie, tearing her at the roots. I help

but not out of his weedy frustration. I collect her in vases

fanning her neatly in our windows, prairie staged for prairie witness.

She reads her reflection in the window like a palm. Her depletion is a whisper

spreading heavy as noonlight, her ghost submerged beneath our lawn.

Father shows me how to spade and pull from the root

but her breezy flowers and fiery grasses swell tuber-thick

in the earth, muscling root-leathers in clay and clay is a firm fist.

And, anyway, prairie roots crowd angry in vases, gripping

their clay fists, claiming the water metallic and mute

as blood. Between her and hers are the grasses stilled in their ghosts.

Petals lapse the lawn-ironed horizon. Heat insists

on the feral scent of grief. I cut the roots. Father cautions me

against discarding them in our flower beds—invasive species

are insistent. In vases, the prairie smells of drowned air, calcifies

the glass, rots overnight, and insists we scry the effluvium

for our morning prayer. Withered stamen, balding ovaries—

How do her petals withstand fists of storm and wind? I remove the death

and change the water, unable to discern her kind of thirsting.

In Front Range News

Deer roaming backyards seduce mountain lions into neighborhoods.

House cats disappeared by coyotes; house cats swooped up by owls.

A dark man, a dark man, a dark man. Drought.

A nest of something buzzing tangled in our yard.

Preposition for Our Belonging

Who scolded us said mint was a weed, told us to control
our heavy yard heaving through the windows, shades rattling the wind—

Immigration haunts me *resemblance*, haunts me how to language *arrival.* I come

to the patterns of swift light, coming to and from, near and too near to here
where the air should smell less like there.

Belonging is shadowboxing with a phantom limb

Seeking love from what I should be. Seeking love from what fears me.

I smell the sweat of this façade—

the false meats of our kitchen, our mortars full of mint.

That we are full of immigrant, our distance storms.

We bathe the breath of our onion ire.
We kindle the hot white hearth.
We bite our tongues laughing.
We decorate the bruises of our fathers' discipline.
We enter and exit wounds
from one to the next—

But I am only half full: half here, half there, and never nearing.

I am a microcosm shadowboxing

as I migrate to my mother's house, full of American

and, furiously, she washes the coconut oil from my hair.

Here or there, I cannot say *we* without meaning *them.*

I weed myself out, a strange overgrowth spreading

between the fences and their homes.

I Move Now to the Exclusion of My Wilderness

You and I, Father—we were often driving. The Friday night me-exchange (Mondays to Mother, Fridays to Father) when through the prairie I tried to tame myself for your home.

The road dusted up and pebbles spit at the windshield, the sun threatening night behind us.

If there were lectures to be given or, if from the previous weekend visit (my time was always *visiting*), there were behavioral critiques to be made, you did so, seriously as secrets, on our Friday night drives.

As you spoke, I watched myself in the window in the mirror.
In the prairie's nocturnal charge, I saw myself far reflected.

I read, *Objects in mirror may be closer then they appear.*
Objects in mirror may be closer then they appear!

As if *what* withholding until *when*. As if *when*, what closeness
might be approaching. As if into *what*, is disappearing.

The prairie held herself nothingly.

What does this mean for objects in mirror? I thought as you spoke me firm against the contours of solitude steadily passing by.

Each object—*May it be already closer?*   *Then, how may I see it appear?*
Then, that moment of appearing!

The night slipping in occasional headlight—

I contemplated the physics, the distance, the possible improbability—*may be*—believing that, in the adult world, all warnings had this kind of poetry.

Once, when you lectured hard, I felt so overcome with rage I opened the door and jumped.

You caught me by the arm, the seatbelt grabbed me like a distance I feared I knew was a limit.

I did not know the distance between *then* and *than*.
The resemblance appeared like a flat tire.

For a moment though, I had seen the road, closer
                    then my fingers blurred into the gravel unfurling, closer
                                        than you called me an idiot—*Idiot! Close the door!*

You called me *Idiot* again and again and again I let that distance watching me watch myself
in the mirror, in the window lecturing me, *appear appear closer appear—*

Grazing on the Nerves of Forgiveness

A neighbor girl asks me why my father is Black—*It's weird that he's Black*, she says.
Why? I ask, my skin shaking like autumn losing
itself to the bones.

•

Home is a material we are wrapped inside—national, domestic, ecological, skin—

The sky bends its blue gaze of surrender.
My father fathers a citizen.

A weed in the concrete, a rupture of fire ants,
the lag lines of evaporating hands.

•

When my father arrived in America, he studied in Atlanta.
America was not as White as he had imagined, he tells my sister and me.

Father decorates our home with sculptures from the Ajanta Caves.
A red velvet chair in which Dayawati loved to knit.
Brass birds flying across the wall.
We listen to Ravi Shankar on record.
Together, we climb a ladder and water the plants heaped above us like, amid this prairie,
a jungle.

•

My father's sisters—my buas—agree, *Everyone loves babies that are fat and White.*
I was skinny and confused.

•

My mother loves the sun so much she says she wants to be a napping cat in her next life. Sometimes when we are reading in the sun, she falls asleep and I fall in love with the sun for loving my mother so sweetly.

•

Rebel son, you are my rebel father—to marry a White woman, an American. To not return home. To divorce.

At the wedding, Dayawati gives my mother her gold bangles, a red sari, and an ivory carving of the Three Wise Monkeys:

See no evil, hear no evil, speak no evil.

•

After my parents' divorce, everyone wants to know
why that sweet, young White woman has such a dark daughter—
I smile so everyone can see my smile is sweet as hers.

After the divorce, everyone looks at us like, *what is that dark man doing with that child*—
I smile and talk to everyone so that my father smiles too.

•

The sun sets and the cul-de-sac swells with grilled meat. But from my house, the intricate embroidery of jeera and burnt onion.

I don't want to eat ketchup dinner at a friend's house, but I am curious about church.

•

My mother tells me my skin is exotic, and that *exotic* means *unique*.

If my skin is exotic, do I feel less
its tensions?

My father tells my mother to keep me out of the sun—
If I am kept from becoming dark, do I?

I love the sun and become what I am.

•

When I play hide-and-seek, I hide in my father's closet. I peek from behind his slacks, transfixed by Dayawati's silver deities, her small gods preserved in silver aura on a silver platter tucked under a curtain of his neatly pressed shirts, next to a bowl of pocket change.

I hide. I close my eyes and don a silver aura. I tremble a ghost hidden in my throat—deadweight jaws, a pea-sized knot under the cushion of my tongue. I am possessed by what I cannot say. I search the sensation like it is a tiny brain inside my mouth. I believe it a prayer, and so I pray.

•

How does one become a cat in their next life? I wonder when Mom and I can't sleep, blocks of light roving wall to wall with the lonely labor of headlights.

We force sleep to toss us a dream before Mom's midnight alarm
and then, the babysitter knocking like a shiver at our door.

•

When anyone speaks of my great grandmother, Malavi Devi,
they begin with the light color of her eyes. They sigh and say *though cruel, beautiful.*
White skin and they remember, until death, her perfect white teeth.
My grandfather had light skin and gloomy blue looming in his eyes.
My father is dark and cringing at this sentence.
His sisters are creamy white.
The eldest has been so cruel, I think she is perhaps a reincarnation of Malavi Devi.
It's karma—this eldest bua explains a dark child's darkness
as negative karma carried from a past life.
Could have been animal abuse, she continues. With pictures and everything.

•

Many times, when I was a child, I was the only dark child.
My rage so confused, so unloved. I carried a closet with me.

My mother calls me prickly, a cactus, a hedgehog, anything with spikes.

The White waiter hands my White kid-cousins a glass of water, *Pass this to your nanny,* she directs them, smiling at me, winking.

I don't correct her—but neither does my whole White family.

•

How to see no evil, how to speak—

I don't know the preposition relating me *here*.

•

My mother calls the umber dots on my skin *beauty marks*.
I count them to see how beautiful I am.

When we can't sleep, she braids my hair and, in the morning, opens it into waves she calls *princess hair.*

Princess, let down your hair, she begs.
I am convinced.

In the fairytale, the lost girl claiming to be a princess is given a bed of a hundred feathered mattresses as a test. When, in the morning, she complains of poor rest, she opens her dress and the bruises on her back prove she isn't lying.

•

Where my father comes from, it's poor to be dark and skinny.
It's working class, like my mother and her family.
My father tells me I am too skinny. He forces me to eat so I eat less and less and less—
The act of chewing makes my skin crawl. I go wild imagining the world digesting inside me.
I fold eggs into roti into napkins. Bury the knot of it in the bin.
I grow into the comfort of hunger—pangs grinning like the sun breaking dawn—
light seething and clear in the heavy appendix of my childhood.
Once, walking down a long hotel hallway lecturing me about breakfast, my father becomes so angry at my thinness, he grabs my waist and shakes me.

I hate writing *stomach* and *belly.*
No belly! the ballet teacher commands, poking there where I wanted most to disappear.
My body is a cave. I echo, echo, echo.

•

After my father's heart attack, an uncle visits us from Delhi. He is a chemist and an Ayurvedic healer and helps us nurse my father back to health. He leads me to a window and asks to see inside my mouth. I swallow, tidy my jaws, and stretch flat the firm cushion of my tongue. He reads. He lifts my tongue and peers underneath. A prayer, the tinnitus in my teeth. *You hold many secrets,* he diagnoses. I shut my mouth full of feathers. I cradle a stutter searching like a lost girl on my tongue. She acts like a smile and she cannot sleep. Something forked flares beneath, a knot frays a grazing brain. Pea-sized bruises button down her back. No one believes her. A surface of tension approaches its peak.

•

My mother is beautiful and has two beautiful daughters: a White daughter and a brown one. She says, *Both my daughters are as beautiful as models.*

Her White model daughter is runway, toothpaste, *Vogue.* But of me she says, *sensual, centerfold, pinup—exotic means unique.*

She is proud of our beauty because each is a version of her own desires.

Between our galaxies of beauty marks, she constellates everything she wants to see
and nothing she hears, nothing
she speaks.

•

In a dream, I'm on stage surrounded by men. Beyond them, at the next stage, a girl dances for no one, but my father is sitting there, eyes turned down at a glass of water.

Men like that never tip, a White girl tells me.

They call us *Dream Girls* and give us T-shirts with an exploding gun.

•

My mother repeatedly tells me girls are smarter than boys, because she knows I'll need to believe it.

•

By the time I am five, my nerves swing on the command to pleasure. I will have to perform things I don't believe.

There is feeling and becoming and then there is belief.

We don't have cable, but I've seen magazines
and recognize my body believed.

I hear the slip and know the charge between *exotic* and *erotic*.

In the police report, I am five and I call it *biting his carrot*. An officer with a pen describes me describing it to him.

•

Many men ask me what I am—I tell them to guess and let their fantasy be correct.

•

In the police report I call it *biting his carrot* and an officer with a pen describes me describing it to him.

The sixteen-year-old White boy on the first floor babysits an apartment complex full of dark girls. My mom and I share a stoop with him. He is number five and we are number six.

I am five going on six.

My back is full of scratches.

I am five and I understand the meaning of looking over my shoulder. I practice it in the mirror.

I practice my eyes.

When will I be sweet sixteen?—I ask the bathwater and count on my fingers.

Under water they fume white like tiny white carrots.

Autumn loses its mind.

If I am ever lost, I ask, *Where are five and six?*

Every kid in this complex has only mothers, it seems, including the boy in number five. I am not sure about the fathers, but I see mine each weekend. He discovers my back full of bruised scratches, traces them under the inspection of bathroom lights, asks me, *What is this?* He pulls them gently open as if inside, the answer.

Because the boy in number five's name was—

I refuse to wear Levi's jeans.

I look over my shoulder. Looking without offending, buffering the threat ever looming.

Four dollars an hour. I wonder, what did Five buy with his babysitting cash?
Or, for what forgiveness did he save it—

•

Of what we resemble to tell, speak no evil.

•

Father brings me with him to his car garage, USA Lube-n-Tune, on the weekends. I arrange the magazines, serve coffee to customers, make bracelets out of printer paper, teach myself Paint, Solitaire, Mahjong on the computer. I drink Dr. Pepper and love the smell of gasoline. I have my first crush on a mechanic named Nicole. Each morning, Nicole gives me her pink sweater to wear while she works. It smells like jasmine and gasoline. *It's cashmere, doll,* she says, sticking her freckled nose in the air, clutching at the heart of her borrowed mechanics jumpsuit where *Steve* is embroidered under the soft white erotic of her engine-greased hands.

•

Growing up, my White cousin and I are close—he is unhinged, and I pretend to like it because no one else puts up with him. I like it because when he is sometimes sweet, he is sweet only to me.

When we are teenagers, he tells me I used to be ugly but now I'm hot, *like a Puerto Rican girl.* He laughs.

One night, he is laying behind me, holding me sweetly then tight, tighter, grabbing my breasts
into fists. I clench
my thighs, hide
between them, a knot. I pretend
to sleep, but am sick
frozen awake all night
I worry, can he hear the feathers fill my chest—O, my belabored creature
stuffed breathless and bruised
beneath his heavy, seamless sleep.

When I tell him I am queer, he calls me a *fucking queer.*

He calls me a *fucking n-word dyke* and laughs maniac laughter.

He marries a White supremacist who only listens to "White music," which is a burned CD of The Rolling Stones and Eminem. He responds to my social media post, *your not a person of color your my cousin* [*sic*]. Emoji laughter.

Years later, he calls me from prison. He's in for domestic violence, can never again contact his wife or children. He's apologizing to me for things he *might have said* in the past.

So, you married a girl, he laughs. *Do you two like cuddle on the couch and watch movies and shit?* he laughs.

I tell him we live by the sea and invite him to come visit whenever he is released.

But he long lost his license and I know how afraid he is to fly.

•

There is anger there
There is anger there
There is anger there
there.

•

My mother calls me *princess* because I am *sensitive to everything*, like *everything* is a tiny, innocuous pea.

•

Speak—No—   Petrified jaw of my deepest discipline: *A saying. A saying.*

Home is where   pressing, pressing mute.   I won't say but when I am outed to my family, I confirm the accusation. A tiny brain drops out of my mouth, desperate as a beetle on its back.

My father cannot forgive this truth, playing dead then scurrying away, glinting like a belief.

Deny it, I am told—for parents' sake, *hide it*. He demands respect, a respectful lie.
He never told his mother about his divorce, he justifies—*An example of respect*, he fumes.

I imagine Dayawati in Delhi, a late noon light, her hands resting on her belly, thinking of her son asleep in America with his family—not alone on the edge of a dark, undone prairie, heating cans of lentil soup, working late on his relentless fight for shared child custody.

Too, I fight for me—

Too, I am alone and desperate—I might not survive more silence, my tongue tied up with truths lying and lies truthing me.

My tongue tied up like a fist, beating each breath bruised and confusing everyone I love away from me.

•

I trace the uneasy poetry of building home—
the manic fret between a flower and her wind.

I graze the nerves of forgiveness—
amnesia rolls in like the fog of a long-distance call.

I try and hear   no evil

but, where are my mothers—
Mothers, where is your daughter?

Grazing the last plot of this feeble, forgiving land.

•

One day we are driving through a congested maze of traffic in Delhi—a man on a bike had been hit by a car. Gridlocked, there is no space to maneuver around him. He is shaking in the street, each car driving gently over, over him—our driver driving slowly over the body.

Why—I speak
like a sieved prayer.

Whoever stops could be blamed, my father, breathless, explains, pulling me back from the window.

Wrapped in rags, children carrying naked babies tap the windshield for money.
Men get out of their cars, encouraging a nursing cow from the road.

See, hear, speak—we pray.

Guilt domesticates mercy—we pray
forgiveness dilutes memory.

But life is decades and decades of traffic.

•

Grasses wheeze at the back of our cul-de-sac. Lightning strikes and ember surrenders ash, signals the urgent mercy of rhizome and rivulet, signals séance of subcutaneous knots, thirty-year seeds of fireweed in bloom.

O Prairie, unforgiving land—some heavy devil weathers my vision skimp—

I become the distance of the world inhabiting my distance.

•

If America isn't as White as expected.

If my father throws the fluffy dice out my car window because they make me look immigrant, un-American.

If my skin is exotic, do I?

•

The mirror unbuttons her blouse to my skin.

•

When a man who has been eyeing me for an hour buys me a drink at the bar—
When we start talking and I answer *No, I don't speak Spanish*—
When he asks me what I am—
When I tell him what
I am.
When he throws the bar stool, yelling *Why the fuck you standing here looking all Mexican and shit?*
And storms out of the bar—

•

I become a fault of neon, a shame-spinning disco ball—
a wound echoing in the eyes of a thousand echoing wounds.

•

The cab driver asks if I know that the meaning of my name is *peace*.
Every time you introduce yourself you say: I am peace, here is peace—he celebrates.

•

I unzip, I pop the clasp. I pull the straps down.

•

When I am outed to my family, my father removes the Ajanta Cave sculptures from our walls and hides them in the basement.

As if, transfixed, my gaze lusted the holy-sensuous curves of devis.

As if, transfixed, I become, seduced by their voluptuous piety.

As if *transfixed* was not a trembling under my tongue, a thing hiding in the closet of my throat.

Call it homoerotic, call it sacred passion, call it possession—

I believed in it.

•

I unbuckle, I loosen the laces. I stretch the tension over my head.

•

I lean in, nakedly. My stage name does not mean *peace*.
On stage I say, *I am fire, here is fire*—
wherein the blue heart of bruise burns hottest.

•

As such, the prairie sharpens her long but pious blades.
As such, she hardens herself at the roots.

And here, the wind cutting herself against the frenzy she bends in the blades.
And hear the grass tongue-tied in the hard, red drought of wound—

O Mercy, laboring creature—
Can I be as the prairie: unforgiving yet pulsing electric her seduction of fireweed
in the pining char of pyre?

•

That violence breaks and breaks between us—we become kaleidoscopic tailspin
binging on the light.
My body wraps me a home of a thousand razor-thin faults.
I appear the preposition of my belonging—

Endless prairie mind

Lone cricket
in the pipes

Home is where
under my soft erotic
I storm

IV

Seduction, after Bark Beetle

Play dead, darkness
caught in the seam
between our lips.

I dance the night into shifts of light, burrow gaze to rot—

Mercy, relay the ways nerve dries into bone

where disorder is something disappearing you
from the inside—

slow, black happiness,
antennal and aglow.

Men come from/for their mothers and go.

I take a fistful of pomegranate to the mouth:

The poem is a stage on which the wound swerves.

Watch, the edge is on fire

and I burn only to survive it.

Psychic neon drawn from the ash

A seduction of prairie cracks the concrete.

Wind sucks herself through the panes of my shelter.

Séance—
Mercy is a seeing, a sprawling sight.

The stage opens its eye. The pyre opens a soliloquy of fire.

Wind turns in dust turning inside the nerves of pious grass, pious to the coyote in convent,
pious to the beetles, black
as my sister's eyes, as between shocks of lightning the window claims me reflected—

Enter, Prairie, with her ancestral wells of pleasure,

her neon ravage of fireweed, her phantom howl
in the fractured trap of animal jaw.

Between the Earth Dreaming Us Out

As swaths of grass sprawled and tethered between telephone poles, I sprawl the stage and tether the gaze.

A man razes my belly with his knuckled machines, a crane lifts away mountains of clay.

In this hollow, here, he will cement a home.

I slip into splits. The prairie appears lithe but her biomass swells below the surface.

Deep roots tether soil from erosion whether I fetal like torrential rain or whirl the dry devils of my leather.

Silt and sand, loess and till—prairie soil is a matrix, larger grains held by finer ones.

I am loom and limb of Dayawati's resurrection.

From her roots, I grow feral gestures. I arch the heavy winds of drought and spit the milk of my weeds.

Where the ruptures of our bodies collect in rivulets, we carve the earth into a wilderness of meandering nerves.

•

One that ties knots. One that unfetters them.

I pry this intimacy with my teeth.

Tender, tearing river, what rots in our mouth, what killing?

•

I am buried in the aspect of body.

Erotics is a protest—yes, crocus!—a signal for survival.

If we could resurrect from the marrow of collapse a tender knot—

But, I begin with Dayawati near the burgeoning pyre.

Hands lay on shoulders, hands laying hands, hands knotted in prayer, hands kneading her body, echo

the obscure and intimate hands of cremation.

Heat is parasitic. The body a conduit for disorder.

Garlands of marigold swoon ablaze and the red wailing of her final sari—

How does fire navigate a body? And when the heart falls, kindling—

The tender knot in which we loop and tether, loop and tether, loop—

•

A seduction, a many-limbed dance. I glide on the heels of a dark night. Watch me watch me in the mirror.

An emptied body is a heavy rope.

My ankles, my wrists bound, my neck.

I lay on my back, lean at the elbows, a slack loop hangs from my ankles. I draw them apart, gaze the riverbed between my legs—I tug taut the knot suspended, strobing like the looped heart of a ghost.

•

Daya wears my body like the prairie wears drought.

I graze a confusion of thirsting nerves. She holds me

like a caught animal, extracting what harm from my mouth—

Eyes or breath? she asks, as if I am one of her suicides.

•

In the ruptured body, desire is synapse without a center.

I ravage the intricacies of weather—eruptions of seduction—I follow astray.

Sometimes, I starve an intentional starvation.

I wander wildernesses toward the divine city of each chakra but retreat,

feeling the compass of my survival seduced.

Pain is a mind in a knot.

I tie my legs to the pole and swing my mind at the stage circumference.

Men lick their lips of ribs.

I draw a heart on a napkin and stint the artery for them.

Time coagulates vertigo in each tiny skull buried in my myofascial prairie.

This is out of body.

I seduce myself into each organ and watch the blood of birds blow by.

•

I have a story that no one will listen.

I show them the twist and bury the gun in my thighs.

But the gun is my fist twisted from being dragged at the wrist.

In the end, the fracture ribbed in my cheek radiates a kiss.

•

The ruptured body is a restoration site trampled by deer into beds.

The most permanent damage I have is performing healing.

This leather trying to make an animal happen slumps into a shoe.

The deer, it appears, are all day all body at the edge of a field barbed with *No Trespassing*—

But then—a cut startles so good.

•

From every ancient bruise, a limb grows, forming a joint with one's reflection.

Every man takes a hand and shakes it, shakes it, shakes it.

•

I perform by way of expressed pressures and currents.

I curl into the late feather of my limbs.

Daya charges the strike and ash of my fire.

I leak the ancient wetness of our wells. I invoke the electric surrender of our rhizome.

A single blade whips in fits.

The landscape hears a glass shatter its waitress.

The heavy heads of still and lusting stems.

My heel is a high tree leaning on a broken limb.

In the mirror, caught light resembles ghosts sinking, sinking in.

•

We gloom the properties of wailing.

We kindle, we feed [on] her cremation.

Winking embers, digital sigh of wet bark. Willful wood and willing. Knots burn long and hot.

Do you fear the hunger of this body?

in obscure communion with intimate patterns.

•

I lift my head and take survey of the land, pocked with clearing, girdled in grid.

A cul-de-sac imagines itself around her neck.

The gnawing at her shoulders is wings that are the hands of men.

Instead of flying, they flip her over and harrow into her, a grave.

Future homes, desires.

Better homes and lawns lawns lawns.

In the striptease, I don the quilt of disappearance.

I lay with my head hanging off the stage, cradled in the hands of a capricious man.

I lay with my head hanging off the stage, legs bent and splayed like giving birth but instead taking.

I perform the headless woman gathering into my womb, miles and miles of red sari.

My hair catches the flame of a candle. Dayawati warms herself by the pyre.

•

When a prairie dies, fungi and bacteria return nutrients to the soil—

I spill a spell of beetles.

My hips sway the crickets' treble.

Hypnosis of unrelenting land, seeds split their bellies, a storm

hails its own demise.

Dayawati unspools herself from the hands of fire.

Her ash spreads and summons the eyes of rhizome.

I rest my hand on the earth's belly, one land kneading the other's silence.

Our tongues split and wander there.

•

Dayawati invokes the electric resurrection of my reflection.

We bite our tongues laughing. I enter the mirror and echo the lips of light.

I see the surface resembling my glitched living. I watch us cross the horizon.

I invoke a rupture of fireweed at the riverbed of our thirsting.

I don the firm shield of beetles. I lick the wound and enter.

I seduce myself to the roots and suck on ancient water.

The land rattles with resilience, the prairie stutters a climax of survival—crocus, yes, crocus!—
I bleed weeds and knot my eyes!

Men spread dollars across the land. A snake seduces each bill, swallows them like mice.

How Any of Us Survived

What body of mine has returned
          a rearview of the prairie, eloping nostalgias.

That the earth is strange
                    and the heart an even stranger,
     a swift low animal for whom you linger, posture to posture

          out of fear of making   quick signal   threatening.
     Out of empathy for   its instinctual trapping.

It's true, what you do
                    is what you mean to each other.

It's true, that what haunts you
                    are those fears given your child   (forgive you)

would you   forgive what hunts you,

what hunts you to make you

hunt.

Ji: A Catalog of Future Mercies

I grew up just really hating him, okay? And I always said that—I said, When, when I have my kids, I'm not going to be like that. I'm going to give everything that I have to my kids. I'm going to give everything I have to my family. *You know? Because I just didn't want to be like him. I said,* I don't want to be anything like that, *you know?*

I.

What fueled us the most, Father—

What trespasses impressed on each other's suffering—

We unfurl our love from ancient angers. We sit in the living room, silent as the tea cooling, in unstuttered smoke. The metal fruit basket glints from the edge off of which I once slammed it, soft apples to the floor.

I understand why you love my sister best. Of anyone, I understand you best.

•

Ji is a moniker of respect used as a suffix, as in Dadi Ji/दादीजी/beloved Grandmother, or Pita Ji/दादाजी/honorable Father.

As a noun, *ji* translates to *heart*, *soul*, *wish*—love in the subjunctive, in recognition of future mercies.

•

Your father, mere Dada Ji/मेरे दादाजी/my grandfather, lived alone in Delhi after Dadi Ji died. He was drinking and in pain; nearly all the money had been gambled and spent, and he had scared the servants away. A doctor came to visit him. The diagnosis was dire: in-home surgery, as soon as possible, would be required.

You pleaded with him to come to America for the operation, but Grandpa loved *India only*.

•

Growing up, I was secretly (or maybe not so secretly) obsessed with India. I mostly imagined into its mystique and asked few questions. From early on you made it clear that you would tell me the information I needed to know, sparing me the complex uneasiness of our situation. You didn't, for example, tell me when you went back to India to remarry. Devastated, I found the pictures a year later, tucked in a drawer. I was jealous of everyone in attendance, but mostly of the little girl my age who was now my cousin, in bindi and bangles, leaning sweetly into my stepmother, such well-behaved daughters.

I was always snooping, elaborating foreign objects into personal narrative. The artifacts in our home allured me: brass vases, stone statues, the erotic twists of tapestry, small, warped records slipped from covers with bombastic Devanagari script above dark, yearning eyes, the scent of sandalwood beaded into my lehenga, an illustrated portrait of Sai Baba that I believed and boasted to friends was of my grandfather, *mere Dada Ji*, humbly I lowered my eyes.

•

When he was manic, your father wore red—you recall his outrageous costumes, Father, especially at school lunchtime—*He'd show up doing stupid things, being funny.* You lower your eyes in memory of your drunk father throwing money. Everyone jumping for coin and laughing—

What has trespassed, Father? Who are the citizens of memory?

When he was depressed, he wore white kurta only. Late into the nights of your childhood, he'd play records full volume on the gramophone. In awe of the telephone—a single sublime sound defining the moment here and elsewhere—he'd ring his older sister in Nagpur and hold the phone to the sound horn, sending Lata's ethereal truths trembling across the lines—

Trembling incoherent distances—trembling incoherent, but true.

You recall your mother crying, you begging your father to sleep. The servants awakened, watching, waiting. Some covering their mouths, laughing.

•

When he woke post-surgery from the anesthesia, Dada Ji was immobilized by a plaster cast entombing him from the hips down, over his feet, and his apartment had been completely emptied. Everything except an unreachable cup of water on a crate next to the bed had been stolen; the "doctor" had left Dada Ji for dead.

For days, you tried to reach him. From America and for days, a trembling unknowing.
For days, the operator reported the requested line dead.

•

It is said that mercy is *like* forgiveness—

What is the distance of resemblance, Father?

And in this distance: pity or pardon— What occasions gratitude? To forgive and—

Amnesia sighs the debt of this resemblance. I tug on the heart of difference. I plead.

•

It wasn't until my late twenties when, in response to my demand for an apology, you raged one loose: *You think my father ever apologized to me?* you implored, *Parents don't apologize to children. My dad tried to kill us—do you think he ever apologized to children?* I'm sorry? *Is that what you want me to say,* I'm sorry?

There are two demands I had never heard you make: *I love you* and *I'm sorry.* I accepted your question as a confession to both, as a commanding of their resemblance.

•

With your sisters also in America, you reached out to your older brother, the stolen son, who lived an hour's flight from Delhi and traveled there frequently on business. But, wanting nothing to do with the family, he refused your plea to check on Dada Ji.

For days, no one came to Dada Ji, lying in his bed, starving, dehydrated, pained, and broken in the apartment swelling with the stench of damp, suffocating skin.

•

Father, I know well the soft couch of your palm. I have seen it many times lifted in pledged threat.

But only once have I opened it's pious heat and pressed there, a prayer.

For recovery, for you to wake with repaired heart. Stinted artery, o mercy—mercy the trying blood of my father.

•

What fueled us the most was shame.

Bits of failed construction.

Is there a karma to rust?

Honorable future heart, how to ration you mercy
from the winter keep of our heart
when already our souls wither on their debts?

•

Finally, Father, you reached in-laws who sent an uncle in Delhi to Dada Ji's apartment. The uncle found your father like death, his white kurta stained with urine, leaking from the cast, not softening it.

Uncle Ji phoned—
the smell was like death, he suggested: take mercy on the resemblance.

You tug on the heart of difference and leave for India on the next available flight.

What, in the debt of this distance, to forgive?

The trembling thirty-hour journey to reach him before—

The hours trembling with a decade earlier when you arrived—
but your mother had already been given to the river.

•

Forgiveness hands-me-down a paralyzed grief. Forgiveness is a dead weight forgetting.

Mercy channels memory, furrows the lines of our palms, laying hands.

Show me, Father, how you lay your hands on the hands that, feeding you, bit.

•

When, after your heart attack, you woke from a four-day coma, you could only speak in Hindi.

Common, the nurse explained, the brain fired up with its earliest memories.

You were a terrified child. Your body curled and cringed like kindle at the flame—

How small, how harmed you felt.

In the dark you pleaded with me.   Was I your mother?

In the dark you screamed, you beheld a giant taller than your father.

Like a lost synapse firing in a tangle of tubes and sheets, you tried to burrow. You pulled everything over your head and for the first time I beheld your member—sacred child, my origin, my tender father, I wept with your fear I knew

and knew a great distance had been shattered. Your legs, thin like mine, shivered. I pulled a blanket over you, feet to hips, and told you we were alright. We were alright—in recovery—and how dare fear try and tremble here.

II.

The weeks constrained in plaster cast paralyzed Dada Ji.
He arrived from India a parcel of reduction, an idol
I was not sure how to worship—if to.

I was eleven and having never known him, I performed what I could imagine of a reverent daughter: lowered eyes, low smile, silence.

Propped on pillows like a lithium bookend, he arrived bedridden, a length too long broken to maneuver.

His excavation corroded the skin, lost body losing
a lost mind, a knot
of leather
fraying.

•

We shared little language—nods, hums—hanji/yes, paanee/water, bas/enough—

The strange blue emptying at the edge of his light brown eyes, stunned
at his suffering:
surviving and surviving and—

Soon, my death. Tomorrow—
he pleaded
for a decade.

Bas bas.
Bas, enough, he prayed.

•

My father and his father and me staring at the prairie for hours: great pondering grasses, dilated stillness.

Slowly, suddenly, for years, miles of neighborhood arriving
wide-eyed as a dial tone.

Dropped line, static channel—

How to confront another's tragedy with one's own?

Mercy is a seeing, a sprawling sight.

•

I watch you, Father, arranging Dadi Ji's silver gods, as she did, on her silver altar on her silver platter with brass bells.

Gently you shine each silver belly with white cloth. Gently, you shine.

•

Between roads and homes, in the yet unmanned tracks of land, huddle prairie dogs, antelope—their perked ears and round-eyed sudden scatter, their tense survival.

Adorable, we stutter from the kitchen table.

We interrogate the window, our eyes veering
with a car's headlights passing
through our reflection.

In this, we witness what death won't come for Dada Ji. What left to see—

His rare blue eyes, miles
of perfect sight.

•

Dada Ji has a dream he never remembers.

The dream is stung with sorrow—we listen—seeds harrowed and puckering
with what of survival.

A fabric, miles of decades long, pours from the eyes of a lucid prairie, preying
the seams of suffering.

Mercy takes a seam ripper, rips a seam
and enters.

•

Are there sounds of pain in the night?
the psychic asks.

Yes, hanji—yes.
we plead.

We pity the karma in the black nutrition of beetles—
the rot that preys, that haunts us to love.

That violence breaks and breaks between us—
shattered glass of strong hands
or trembling ones.

Relief appears a shadowed dimension—
Night wailing: Dada Ji brutal as a prairie wind

From a distant corner of the home—
the psychic sees
night split like a phantom
limb of lightning—

No, no pain, he says in the morning.
No, no memory, he rubs his mute legs.

III.

A mind is a tantrum of light turned opaque. Between us, a grief
of subcutaneous knots. Memory claims each emptiness in the thick nerves
of our distance, a ghost town in the sprawl of asthmatic grasses,

collapses—Resemblance: what of my sight is not our species shared?
We enter and exit wounds—one to the next—a garland, rudraksha,
many faces of the same many-faced fruit. The ruptured body

is a restoration site. Where grief roots, drought blooms
milkweed, fireweed, those neon ghosts,
those voracious prayers, antennal and spurred.

•

Father, how tenderly you affix flame to incense.
How quickly you blow and blow it out. How nimbly
you assign it to the altar. How electric
its bindi deifies the smoke.

IV.

How to weigh a hand for its mercy—
late feather of my limbs, a low storm in every joint.

•

In his wheelchair, Dada Ji folds his laundry, stacking the white closet with white kurta only.
In his head, he kneads a knot the size of his brain.

I call him to the kitchen to peel potatoes.
I never call him *Dada Ji*.

To us, the downstairs bedroom is "Grandpa's room," and when in the mornings we find the light switched on, we know there's been a haunting.

•

Are there sounds of pain—

We fold in on ourselves the shuttered questions of ourselves.
We twist into knits like old news we twist
into kindling.

Yes—

The ruptured body is a restoration site kneaded by deer into beds.

Mercy is a deer
and each bed, an altar.

•

He wails in the night, a brutal prairie wind, trembling
tall grass leaning like belonging into fences,
fences neck and neck with the wind, brutal,
our love, a strange overgrowth spreading.

It is, the psychic sees, *Dayawati—*
come to offer mercy.

•

At the foot of his bed, her ghost
summons his lamentations, electric
surrender, we listen
an excruciating excavation.

His soul cannot depart so heavy,
the psychic affirms, mapping with her finger
on our palms, a spiral
like a wound
we enter.

•

Mercy holds in the palm of her heart the hearts of our many-hearted rhizome,
sprawling with the eyes of her third sight, wherein sun
radiates from root to the pistil of her throat—blooms a clarity, a calm fruit.

Dayawati whispers to me the meaning of my name and hands me the end of the rope.

The rope transforms into a garland of rudraksha, dried stone fruit strung around her neck.

We are many faces of the same many-faced fruit and, in the pit of each, a prayer, larval
and aglow.

O
fleshy rib of rhizome
sprout my tongue
acres of antennae

Listen the tall grass
listening

•

Ji—I trace your sorrows a constellation.
I summon your violences, knead altars
for each next to mine. Mercy—our survival,
our love in the subjunctive. I weigh a hand for its grief
and read the knot of lines between us.

Our hands weave a signal cracks
the concrete. I watch my sister's eyes
watch mine. We watch each the horizons
electric behind us. Our hands,
like the prairie-sway of soft blades, rest
on the silver belly of night.

Notes and Acknowledgments

Throughout *A Catalog of Future Mercies*, the image of grass cracking the concrete is inspired by the same image and its corresponding ideas in Lisa Robertson's book *Occasional Work and Seven Walks from the Office for Soft Architecture*.

Thanks to Kachine Kulick for the photo that appears on page 56.

The phrase "Willful wood and willing," from "Between the Earth Dreaming Us Out" is inspired by ideas from Divya Victor's essay ">>[WOMAN WAILING]: On the Problem of Representing Trauma as a Brown Woman Within the Institution of Poetry," which is in conversation with Sara Ahmed's lecture "Snap! Feminist Moments, Feminist Movements."

The book's conception of resilience via erotic empowerment and agency is indebted to Audre Lorde's work at large, but particularly her essay "Uses of the Erotic: The Erotic as Power." The "Seduction" poems in this book as well as "Between the Earth Dreaming Us Out" are dedicated to Lorde.

•

The memoir elements of this book are based on my experience. Certain names have been changed, and certain quotes have been reconstructed from memory to the best of my ability.

Thank you to my family for their continuous love, patience, and support. I am grateful for the ways we have cultivated resilience and joy.

I am particularly grateful to my father and stepmother for always demonstrating the importance of sharing family history. This book is a tribute to your ardent, honest, and compassionate storytelling. Thank you to my sister for organizing and digitally archiving nearly eighty years of family photos—this book was inspired and braced by the impeccable archive you created. And thank you to my father for his photographs—it is an exquisite gift to encounter your stories also through your lens.

Thank you to my mother and stepfather for coming to my readings and encouraging the passion you saw in me from a young age. Thank you to my sisters for your unshakable love and care—your hearts are my most sacred homes.

A Catalog of Future Mercies is dedicated to my grandmother, Dayawati. Each hour spent in communion with this book is in honor of your life and in recognition of your relentless spirit.

To my grandfather, Anand—I miss your phone calls, I miss cutting your hair. I miss sitting with you in deep, calm surrender. Thank you for those quiet moments.

To my teacher, Julie Carr—thank you for your love, your keen advice, and for demonstrating—in your work and life—the symbiosis between intelligence and vulnerability, which was crucial to my discovery and legitimization of my vision and voice.

To my teacher, Selah Saterstrom—thank you for your love, support, and wisdom. I am especially grateful for the imperative wisdom you imparted to me for this book: "Find clarity in the multivalence." It is an honor to write in communion with your body of work and to learn from your deep commitment to love.

Eternal gratitude to my fierce companion in this institution of poetry, Divya Victor. Your mind and heart have held me in innumerable ways, and your wisdom has ferried me through these pages. Your work and thinking have been imperative for this book, as has your encouragement and advice. Thank you for your laughter, your voice memos, your endless support, and your vital contemplations.

The final iteration of this book would not have been possible without the sharp mind and tender wisdom of Tesha Zietlow. Thank you for reading endless drafts, talking though tough revisions, taking excellent author photos, and cooking delicious meals. Your love, brilliance, and attention nurtured and refined the spirit of this book.

Martha Ryan, thank you for being an early reader of the book and for simultaneously holding me through tough life moments. This book is indebted to you in more ways that I can list here. Thank you for continually bringing me clarity, breath, care, and laughter. Thank you for always reaching out and showing up. Your friendship is rare and profound, and you are the funniest person I know.

Jaclyn Baca Carroll, thank you for being my first friend and my cosmic kin. I dedicate this book to us, to the inquisitive, spunky little girls trying to understand ourselves and the world from Aurora, Colorado. This book would not have been possible without your strength, spirituality, and endless love—you were with me every moment of its making. It is a joyous honor to move through this life with you.

Kachine Kulick, you ignite the sensual magic pulsing through this book. I have composed many of these poems on a dance floor, alongside you. Thank you for standing in your erotic power and for witnessing me in mine.

For their fearless scholarship and holistic wisdom, I am eternally grateful to Page Valentine Regan. Thank you for teaching alongside me in these dynamic times. You are the twin flame of my mind.

Andrew Houchens, thank you for your epic friendship and love. To be in art and companionship with another person for so many decades is a rare gift. This book is indebted to the art you showed me, to the places you explored with me, to the liberation you opened in me—thank you.

I am incredibly grateful to Piper J. Daniels and Lila Bonow for being early readers of this manuscript. Thank you for holding this work in its most vulnerable, raw, and messy form. And thank you for making work that is in kinship with this book—such relationships are a profound and luminous way of keeping in company.

Deepest gratitude to Prageeta Sharma for your beautiful friendship. Your care, love, honesty, and integrity have transformed me. Thank you for being a light for me even in your darkest moments. Thank you for showing me how to surrender without suppressing my fire.

Thank you to HR Hegnauer for many dear years of friendship and for designing an incredible professional website for me.

Nicholas Gulig, Sommer Browning, Kazim Ali, Alicia Mountain, Teresa Carmody, and Aditi Machado, thank you for your friendship and for your work, which continually inspires me.

Thank you to Jeffrey Pethybridge and the Jack Kerouac School of Disembodied Poetics for always supporting me and my work. Thank you to Anne Waldman for being the first poet to illuminate poetic channeling and performance for me, decades ago. Thank you to Ed Bowes, for your films and for letting me be inside them, where I discovered new realms of art making.

Thank you to Ian Leonard for your friendship and for your precise and animated transcriptions of family interviews, which comprise the backbone of this book.

I am incredibly grateful for the editorial brilliance at Graywolf. Immense gratitude to Carmen Giménez for believing in the mammoth mess of a manuscript I initially sent—your insistence, patience, and encouragement were vital to focusing and sustaining the spirit of this book. I am eternally grateful for your integrity and vision, and for guiding me to trust the form. Brittany Torres Rivera, thank you for your keen and precise editorial eye—this book is indebted to the clarity you seamlessly sculpt into the fine moments of syntax. Thank you to Jeff Shotts for your invaluable feedback, which empowered the book's final transformations. Thank you to the talented Luis Vázquez O'Neill for designing the book's striking cover. I am overcome with endless gratitude to the entire Graywolf team for the time, energy, focus, and care you put into bringing this book into the world.

Thank you to the Fulbright Program for supporting my yearlong research in India for this book. Additionally, my time in India is indebted to the generosity of Francis and Margaret

Machado, who hosted me for amazing dinners, helped me locate my father's childhood home, and battled hours of traffic to bring me there. Thank you to Siddarth Machado for taking me on an unforgettable adventure in the Western Ghats where I learned—significantly for this book—about cobras.

I am endlessly thankful to Calderwood Studio, a sanctuary at MacDowell, where I completed the first draft of *A Catalog of Future Mercies* alongside the ghost of Jean Valentine, to whom I am also grateful.

Thank you to the editors at *Burrow Press Review*, *Action Books*, *Sink Review*, and *Foglifter* for publishing selections of this work in different iterations. Thank you to Belladonna* Collaborative for publishing an earlier version of "Between the Earth Dreaming Us Out" as a chaplet. Thank you to Tom Brosseau, host of NPR's *The Great American Folk Show*, for featuring me reading poems from the book. And immense gratitude to Shin Yu Pai for the opportunity to speak about the conceptual underpinnings of the book on her podcast, *Ten Thousand Things*.

Thank you to my Denver and Seattle writing communities who, through readings and drafts and courses, have witnessed the development of this book.

I am eternally grateful to my Seattle community of friends—thank you for supporting me and for celebrating with me. This book is indebted to your care, compassion, karaoke, and joy.

To all my students near and far, thank you for your brilliant discussions and for sharing your smart, raw, empowered, and dynamic work with me. Your contributions to our classroom communities have been an imperative part of this book's journey.

I am grateful to the National Endowment for the Arts and to Seattle University for fellowships that supported *A Catalog of Future Mercies*.

Eternal love and gratitude to the two cats, Sammie and Clove, who dreamed next to the book as it was being written.

Finally, thank you to my dance teacher, Gabriel Masson, who, yelling over the music, encouraged us—"If you only think about the steps, you're going to miss the momentum!"

SERENA CHOPRA is a writer, dancer, filmmaker, and performance artist. She is the recipient of an NEA Creative Writing Fellowship and is a MacDowell Fellow, a Kundiman Fellow, a Fulbright Scholar, and an alumna RedLine Resident Artist. Chopra is an associate professor of creative writing at Seattle University.

Graywolf Press publishes risk-taking, visionary writers who transform culture through literature. As a nonprofit organization, Graywolf relies on the generous support of its donors to bring books like this one into the world.

This publication is made possible, in part, by the voters of Minnesota through a Minnesota State Arts Board Operating Support grant, thanks to a legislative appropriation from the arts and cultural heritage fund. Significant support has also been provided by other generous contributions from foundations, corporations, and individuals. To these supporters we offer our heartfelt thanks.

To learn more about Graywolf's books
and authors or make a tax-deductible donation,
please visit www.graywolfpress.org.

The text of *A Catalog of Future Mercies* is set in Sabon Next LT Pro.
Book design by Rachel Holscher.
Composition by Bookmobile Design & Digital
Publisher Services, Minneapolis, Minnesota.
Manufactured by Sheridan on acid-free,
30 percent postconsumer wastepaper.